STUDY GUIDE for BEAUTY BEYOND THE THORNS

STUDY GUIDE

for

BEAUTY BEYOND THE THORNS

DISCOVERING GIFTS
IN SUFFERING

DARCI J. STEINER, MS

Beauty Beyond the Thorns: Discovering Gifts in Suffering

Copyright © 2021 by Darci J. Steiner

All rights reserved. No part of this publication may be reproduced, distributed, or transmitted in any form or by any means, including photocopying, recording, or other electronic or mechanical methods, without the prior written permission of the publisher, except in the case of brief quotations embodied in critical reviews and certain other noncommercial uses permitted by copyright law.

Published in Parker, Colorado, by Darci J. Steiner.

Although the author/publisher have made every effort to ensure that the information in this book was correct at press time, the author/publisher do not assume and hereby disclaim any liability to any party for any loss, damage, or disruption caused by errors or omissions, whether such errors or omissions result from negligence, accident, or any other cause.

Adherence to all applicable laws and regulations, including international, federal, state, and local governing professional licensing, business practices, advertising, and all other aspects of doing business in the US, Canada or any other jurisdiction is the sole responsibility of the reader and consumer.

Neither the author nor the publisher assumes any responsibility or liability whatsoever on behalf of the consumer or reader of this material. Any perceived slight of any individual or organization is purely unintentional. The resources in this book are provided for informational purposes only and should not be used to replace the specialized training and professional judgment of a health care or mental health care professional. Please always consult a trained professional before making any decision regarding treatment of yourself or others.

All Scripture quotations, unless otherwise indicated, are taken from the Holy Bible, New International Version®, NIV®. Copyright © 1973, 1978, 1984, 2011 by Biblica, Inc.™ Used by permission of Zondervan. All rights reserved worldwide. www.zondervan.com. The "NIV" and "New International Version" are trademarks registered in the United States Patent and Trademark office by Biblica, Inc.™, Inc.™

Scripture quotations marked (RSV) are from the Revised Standard Version of the Bible, copyright © 1946. 1952, and 1971 National Council of the Churches of Christ in the United States of America. Used by permission. All rights reserved.

All emphases in Scripture quotations have been added by the author.

Author Photos by @GlennAsakawa
Cover Design and formatting by Alejandro Martin
Editor April Alvis www.aprilalvis.com
Editor Kassidi Sikes www.kassidisikesediting.com
Author Website www.DarciJSteiner.com

Paperback ISBN: 978-1-7376031-0-8
eBook ISBN: 978-1-7376031-1-5
Study Guide ISBN: 978-1-7376031-2-2

Library of Congress Control Number: 2021918695

To my Father in Heaven
who has shown himself to me in profound ways
through the thorn of a disability.
I am truly grateful.

Available on Amazon!

Beauty Beyond the Thorns: Discovering Gifts in Suffering and the *Study Guide for Beauty Beyond the Thorns: Discovering Gifts in Suffering* are best utilized together.

Website: www.darciJSteiner.com

CONTENTS

Welcome

Chapter 1 — 1
The Gift of Hope – My Journey

Chapter 2 — 3
The Gift of Perseverance – Keep Reaching

Chapter 3 — 5
The Gift of Compassion – Unexpected Blessings

Chapter 4 — 7
The Gift of Deliverance – Not Through Man's Ingenuity

Chapter 5 — 9
The Gift of Love – Better Than a Hallmark Love

Chapter 6 — 11
The Gift of Grace – Divine Intervention

Chapter 7 — 12
The Gift of Courage – He Didn't Run Away

Chapter 8 — 17
The Gift of Joy – Unleashed Gratitude

Chapter 9 — 19
The Gift of Community – Air Pocket

Chapter 10 — 21
The Gift of Transformation – A Caregiver's Perspective

Chapter 11 — 23
The Gift of Faith – A Meteorologist's Faith

Chapter 12 — 26
The Gift of Mercy – Mr. Miyagi

Chapter 13 — 27
The Gift of Repentance – Walking Toward the Cross

Chapter 14 — 29
The Gift of Endurance – Purer Than Gold

Chapter 15 — 31
The Gift of Direction – Dirt Roads

Chapter 16 — 32
The Gift of Fulfillment – Food and Addictions Do Not Fulfill

Chapter 17 — 36
The Gift of Provision – Exponential Multiplication

Chapter 18 — 38
The Gift of a Shepherd – Jesus Rescues Cast Sheep

Chapter 19 — 41
The Gift of Touch – Lepers

Chapter 20 — 44
The Gift of Gratitude – One Leper

Chapter 21 — 46
The Gift of a Good Samaritan – Inconvenient Love

Chapter 22 — 48
The Gift of Forgiveness – A Thirty Year Prayer

Chapter 23 — 50
The Gift of Sight – The God Who Sees

Chapter 24 — 52
The Gift of Wholeness – The Only One in the World

Chapter 25 — 55
The Gift of Obedience

Chapter 26 — 61
The Gift of Light – Good and Evil

Chapter 27 — 64
The Gift of Trust – Job Never Knew the "Why"

Chapter 28 — 66
The Gift of Adoration – Receiving Love

Chapter 29 — 68
The Gift of Empathy – A Father, a Counselor, and a Big Brother

Chapter 30 — 70
The Gift of Brokenness – Jesus

Inspirational Quotes from *Beauty Beyond the Thorns* — 72-84

Your Reflections pages — 85-87

About the Author

Welcome!

I'm so glad you are here! This *Study Guide for Beauty Beyond the Thorns: Discovering Gifts in Suffering* is intended to be used alongside the *Beauty Beyond the Thorns: Discovering Gifts in Suffering* book to help you discover gifts God has for you that may seem hidden behind your suffering. Sometimes it takes only a small shifting of our focus to see something good right in front of us—yes, even during suffering.

Suffering provides the resistance we need to grow. If we never suffered, we'd stay the same. Suffering is for our benefit, or God wouldn't allow it. He has a perfect plan for you. If you are experiencing a thorn of pain due to divorce, injury, addiction, grief, loss, depression, infertility, financial trouble, job loss, relationship struggles, etc., you are in the right place. *Beauty Beyond the Thorns* was birthed from loss—the loss of my father, the loss of my ability to walk, and the loss of my independence.

After these losses, I didn't have direction. I was spiraling down in hopelessness. But God gave me the gift of hope through disability which created space for me to write. Writing has helped me work through much of my pain, and in doing so, I found many more gifts God was holding out to me. I believe the same will be true as you write out your thoughts in this study guide. If you don't have a copy of the *Beauty Beyond the Thorns: Discovering Gifts in Suffering* book, I'd encourage you to get one to read alongside this study guide. You can use the two books together in a variety of ways:

1. With a Bible study group, support group, or book club
2. By yourself with God
3. With a friend or two
4. With a spouse or partner

Since there are thirty chapters, you can study one chapter per day for a month. If you are working through the book and study guide with a group that meets weekly, each member can study one chapter per day, then at your weekly meeting you can discuss the chapters read that week. These books can be used in any way that works best for your situation. There is no rush to work through the book in a month; it's merely a suggestion.

I pray you find strength here and discover beautiful gifts God provides to help you through your trials. You have not been abandoned in your suffering. He never leaves you nor forsakes you. "It is the Lord who goes before you; he will be with you, he will not fail you or forsake you; do not fear or be dismayed" (Deut. 31:8).

Blessings,

Darci

Chapter 1 – The Gift of Hope

My Journey

"How can we understand hope without having faith?"

Read chapter 1 of *Beauty Beyond the Thorns*.

Throughout your trial, when all hope seems gone, know that it isn't. It never is. There is more to your story than what your eyes can see or mind can understand. Choose to see your life differently by shifting your focus to reframe your situation. Now look through a spiritual lens to find blessings within your trial. When your life does not go according to plan, try holding on to these beliefs:

- There are new opportunities and ways to grow in this trial. This is a fresh beginning.

- God has something beautiful for me beyond this thorn, which will be revealed to me in time.

- God is working his plan for my life, and his plans are perfect.

- I am worth far more to God than what I can see or feel.

- My family, friends, and other people around me want and need me. I will allow them to love and/or serve me.

- Hindsight will reveal gifts in my suffering.

- I am being formed into who God intends for me to become.

1. Reflect on the points above. Write your new thoughts of hope below.

_____

_____

Q: *"Hoping for something is different than making a wish. Hope is rooted in faith. Hope comes from God; a wish comes from our desires."* – Darci J. Steiner

2. Hope is a gift given to us by God which becomes more secure as we grow closer to him. Read these verses on hope. Choose one to write on a 3x5 card to look at daily until you have it memorized.

   - Against all **hope**, Abraham in hope believed and so became the father of many nations, just as it had been said to him, "So shall your offspring be." Without weakening in his faith, he faced the fact that his body was as good as dead—since he was about a hundred years old—and that Sarah's womb was also dead (Rom. 4:18–19).

   - Not only so, but we also glory in our sufferings, because we know that suffering produces perseverance; perseverance, character; and character, hope. And hope does not put us to shame, because God's love has been poured out into our hearts through the Holy Spirit, who has been given to us (Rom. 5:3–5).

   - Be joyful in **hope**, patient in affliction, faithful in prayer (Rom. 12:12).

   - May the God of **hope** fill you with all joy and peace as you trust in him, so that you may overflow with hope by the power of the Holy Spirit (Rom. 15:13).

   - Let us hold unswervingly to the **hope** we profess, for he who promised is faithful (Heb. 10:23).

Chapter 2 – The Gift of Perseverance

Keep Reaching

"How can we know what perseverance is until we have run out of strength?"

Read chapter 2 of *Beauty Beyond the Thorns*.

We learn perseverance through trials. Perseverance is a gift from God that helps us endure our next trial.

The woman in the Bible who bled for twelve years and was societally marginalized never gave up. When Jesus came to town she persevered to get to Jesus. She wasn't worried about making others unclean; she wanted to be made whole. She knew who to go to and made a beeline to get to him. She didn't want to create a scene; she just wanted to touch him—even if just the fringe of his cloak—and knew he would make her well.

1. Jesus stopped when he felt the power of her faith, and he turned to her with some very good news! Read each of these accounts in the Bible to get a full picture of her story. Notate what stands out to you in each account.

    ➢ Matthew 9:20–22

    ➢ Mark 5:25–34

    ➢ Luke 8:43–48

2. How are you persevering through your trial(s)? Some days may be harder than others, but to persevere you must get up and do everything you know to do. Sometimes we know what we need to do to take a step forward, but we neglect doing so. If you are

neglecting the little things that may help you, begin implementing them. Make a list of the little things, or steppingstones, that can help you get unstuck:

- ➢
- ➢
- ➢
- ➢
- ➢
- ➢

3. Do one of the things on your list today. This is perseverance. You keep going one step at a time. Then on to the next. Do what you know you need to be doing that will help you.

Nothing will help you persevere more than being close to Jesus.

4. Download a Bible app onto your phone. Go ahead—if you'd like, you can do it right now and take some time to get familiar with it. Then, when you feel stuck, make a beeline to Jesus. He has good news waiting for you.

One Moment,

One Steppingstone,

One Day at a time leads to progress.

Progress leads to outcomes.

Chapter 3 – The Gift of Compassion

Unexpected Blessings

"How can we know what compassion is until we've emulated it to the degree Jesus exemplified it?"

Read chapter 3 of *Beauty Beyond the Thorns*.

In the Bible, there was an invalid who laid by a pool for thirty-eight years (John 5:1–15). He was stuck in more than one way. He was an excuse maker. But Jesus had compassion on him anyway. Jesus loves all of us and does not want us to stay stuck.

Throughout my disability, I have also made excuses. I didn't want to use a wheelchair because I didn't want others seeing me in it. I was embarrassed. But by not getting one I was holding myself back from getting better. After four months of persistence, my counselor convinced me to use one. My wheelchair helped free me, not confine me.

1. Do you think watching me use a wheelchair helped my daughters develop compassion for others also using wheelchairs? If it applies, how can you help your children become more compassionate toward those with disabilities? How can you? Discuss or ponder this.

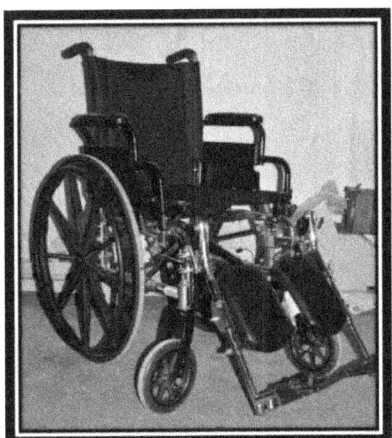

2. We don't know what troubles other people are going through—how they are stuck. What if our compassion is what helps them to move forward and gain hope? Practice having compassion today, wherever you are, including in the car! Then come back and write what you learned.

_____
_____
_____
_____

3. Read these verses about compassion.

    ➢ Jesus called his disciples to him and said, "I have **compassion** for these people; they have already been with me three days and have nothing to eat. I do not want to send them away hungry, or they may collapse on the way" (Matt. 15:32).

    ➢ So he got up and went to his father. "But while he was still a long way off, his father saw him and was filled with **compassion** for him; he ran to his son, threw his arms around him and kissed him (Luke 15:20).

    ➢ Praise be to the God and Father of our Lord Jesus Christ, the Father of **compassion** and the God of all comfort (2 Cor. 1:3).

    ➢ When Jesus landed and saw a large crowd, he had **compassion** on them, because they were like sheep without a shepherd. So he began teaching them many things (Mark 6:34).

4. List of as many synonyms as you can for the word compassion.

5. How can you be intentional about looking at others with a heart of compassion, and acting on that compassion?

    _____
    _____
    _____
    _____
    _____
    _____

Chapter 4 – The Gift of Deliverance

Not Through Man's Ingenuity

"How can we know what it means to be delivered until we've surrendered?"

Read chapter 4 of *Beauty Beyond the Thorns*.

When the Israelites were wandering in the desert for forty years, God had a plan. He didn't have them cross directly from Point A in Egypt to Point B in Canaan. Instead, he took them on a circuitous route to teach them he was trustworthy.

Sometimes we aren't given an easy path, and we find ourselves wandering in circles. I am amazed at how many things in my life I have to do twice—rewrite an article because my computer wigged out, return an item I ordered because the company sent me the wrong item, become disabled twice.

I never dreamed after my first disability I'd become disabled *again*. Just because I went through something traumatic once doesn't exempt me from experiencing trauma again. I am wandering in the wilderness again. But good things come after wandering, if you trust God.

1. Read Matt. 4. What transpired from Jesus' life after he was in the wilderness? Read Matt. 3. What about John the Baptist?

2. What has transpired in your life *after* wandering in the wilderness?

3. What current life events make you feel like you are wandering, not making progress, or even experiencing setbacks from the progress you had made? Make a list below.

   1.

   2.

   3.

   4.

4. Pray for deliverance from each circumstance.

Remember, the timing of deliverance is determined by God, but take some time to pray to learn what he wants to show you while you are in the desert.

Q: *Your pain may be what is delivering you from an even deeper sorrow.*
   – Darci J. Steiner

It may seem like you are traveling in circles in your circumstance, but you may be making your way to your Promised Land!

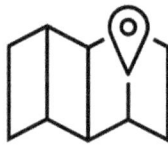

Chapter 5 – The Gift of Love

Better Than a Hallmark Love

"How can we know what love is without allowing ourselves to receive it?"

Read chapter 4 of *Beauty Beyond the Thorns*.

Have you ever watched a Hallmark movie, or two, or three?

Throughout each movie you may have noticed something happens to keep the new love relationship from working out. But then, suddenly, a misunderstanding is cleared up and the stars align!

I met my Hallmark man on a group date when we were on dates with other people. Mark and I were seated together at a table while our dates prepared a Moroccan meal in the kitchen. He called me the following week. Don't worry, neither of our dates were serious—just friends.

Most of the time, Hollywood does not depict the deep nitty-gritty in relationships. When trials come, a cup of hot chocolate, baking cookies together, or going ice skating do not resolve relationship problems as the Hallmark movies would have you think.

Q: Augustine, in *On Christian Doctrine*, says, *"But living a just and holy life requires one to be capable of an objective and impartial evaluation of things: to love things, that is to say, in the right order, so that you do not love what is not to be loved, or fail to love what is to be loved, or have a greater love for what should be loved less, or an equal love for things that should be loved less or more, or a lesser or greater love for things that should be loved equally."*[1]

In other words, how do you order your loves?

Does your life show you love your husband or wife more than your work?

Does your life show that you love your kids more than your friends or phone?

Do you love God? Where is he placed according to how you live your life?

Include work, kids, spouse, job, hobbies, God, and friends.

1. In the first column list your loves here according to *how you live your life*. In the second column, rearrange your loves according to how they *should be prioritized*.

1.	1.
2.	2.
3.	3.
4.	4.
5.	5.
6.	6.
7.	7.

Chapter 6 – The Gift of Grace

Divine Intervention

"How can we understand grace until we've realized our profound need for forgiveness?"

Read chapter 6 of *Beauty Beyond the Thorns*.

I have some relationships in my life I wish I could do over. I have to take the lessons I've learned from making mistakes in the past and prioritize better in the present. We don't get do-overs with most relationships. But even though we mess up, we can receive grace from God, if we follow him. He forgives us. Knowing that he forgives us can help us to forgive ourselves and other people. Forgiveness is grace.

1. Name people you've hurt and desire *forgiveness from* (even those who have passed on). If someone on your list has passed on, God can grant you forgiveness. You aren't left hopeless. Ask him to help you. Talk together about this if you are in a group setting or spend some time alone reflecting and praying for God to lead you to accepting or receiving forgiveness.

2. Who has hurt you that *you* can offer *grace and forgiveness* to? You don't even need to set up a conversation. They may not even know they hurt you. Or maybe there was a complete misunderstanding. It works both ways. We hurt others; others hurt us. Pray to see how God leads you.

Chapter 7 – The Gift of Courage

He Didn't Run Away

"How can we know what courage is until we do something beyond our capabilities?"

Read chapter 7 of *Beauty Beyond the Thorns*.

Caleb is an extremely courageous and faithful man in the Old Testament. Because of Caleb's faith, the wandering Israelites could finally enter the Promised Land.

1. Read the story below about the courage and faith of Caleb:

WHEN ONE MAN BELIEVES

In the book of Numbers, chapters 13 and 14, is a story of wholehearted faith and its opposite, faithlessness.

When the Israelite community was in reach of Canaan, the Promised Land, Caleb, an Israelite leader, was sent by Moses as a spy to explore the land with eleven other leaders/spies. They went up through the Negev and came to the land of Hebron. For forty days, they assessed the strength of the people, the goodness of the land, the fertileness of the soil, and the quality of the vegetation. When they returned, they reported what they saw. All twelve agreed the land "flow[s] with milk and honey," (13:27) and they brought back fruit to prove it.

However, not all agreed the land could be seized. The majority focused on what they *saw* instead of what they heard God promising for forty years. Ten of the twelve leaders saw large, fortified cities and large, powerful people who were descendants of Anak (Anakites) in Hebron—men of great stature who brought fear to those who encountered them. Ten of the Israelite leaders were afraid of them, two were not.

Caleb heard the promise of God ringing in his ear instead of fearing the obstacles he saw. Caleb stood and silenced the people before Moses. He said, "We should go up and take possession of the land, for **we can certainly do it**" (13:30).

The next word in the Bible is "But," spoken by the other leaders who spied out the land. They said, "We can't attack those people; they are stronger than we are" (13:31). They spread a negative, unfaithful report to the Israelites, who were waiting for God's promise to come true—that he would bring them *into* the Promised Land. But most of the leaders weren't leading; they were spreading fear. They said to everyone, "We seemed like grasshoppers in our own eyes, and we looked the same to them" (13:33).

So, with that report, the whole community lost hope and wept and grumbled against God. The Israelites wanted to go back to Egypt (where they were slaves). Moses and Aaron fell face down in front of the assembly. Joshua (one of the twelve spies) and Caleb tore their clothes and stated to the crowd, "If the Lord is pleased with us, he will lead us into that land, a land flowing with milk and honey, and will give it to us. Only do not rebel against the LORD. And do not be afraid of the people of the land because *we* will swallow them up. Their protection is gone, but the LORD is with us. Do not be afraid of them" (14:8-9).

But the Israelite people considered stoning Joshua, and Caleb because they were in the minority. They didn't follow the crowd of whiners and complainers into disbelief.

Then the glory of the LORD appeared at the Tent of Meeting. "How long will these people treat me with contempt? How long will they refuse to believe in me, in spite of all the miraculous signs I have performed among them?" (14:11).

God wanted to destroy the Israelites for their continual faithlessness, sin, and grumbling over their forty years in the desert. But Moses spoke up on behalf of the Israelites, asking God to forgive them. The Lord agreed to forgive them but said to the disbelieving people, "I will do to you the very things I heard you say: in the desert, your bodies will fall—every one of you twenty years old or more who was counted in the census and who has grumbled against me. Not one of you will enter the land I swore with uplifted hand to make your home, except Caleb son of Jephunneh and Joshua son of Nun. As for your children that you said would be taken as plunder, I will bring them in to enjoy the land you have rejected. But you—your bodies will fall in this desert. Your children will be shepherds here for forty years, suffering for your unfaithfulness, until the last of your bodies lies in the desert ... I will surely do these things to this whole wicked community, which has *banded together* against me" (14:28–33, 35).

Because of the ten leaders' and their followers' faithlessness, they were struck down and died. Only Joshua, Caleb, and those 19 years and younger survived. Two of the ten leaders led with belief in God's promises *and didn't let their eyes deceive them from believing what they heard God promise.* They believed the LORD would keep his word no matter the obstacles. God had indeed brought them to the Promised Land, and surely, he would help them possess it.

Moses and Aaron also did not enter Canaan because of their rebellion against God's command at the waters of Meribah. God told Moses to *speak* to the rock to provide water for the thirsty Israelites. Instead, he *struck* the rock. In doing so, he dishonored the Lord in the sight of the Israelites by disobeying the Lord's command.

Even if we are regarded as grasshoppers by people, or feel like a grasshopper facing obstacles, we must remember Caleb's words, "we will swallow them up." "We can do this," Caleb believed, and he did. Sometimes God uses one believer to change the direction of the future for others when s/he believes the Lord is with them. The key? Belief that God will fulfill each of his promises. God had already promised many years prior that he would give them victory and take them into Canaan. But most of the leaders and people forgot.

Forty-five years later, Caleb was given the land of Hebron as an inheritance, as he is the one who drove from it the large and strong three sons of Anak (Anakites). "Now then, just as the LORD promised, he has kept me alive for forty-five years …. So here I am today, eighty-five years old! I am still as strong today as the day Moses sent me out; I'm just as vigorous to go out to battle now as I was then. Now give me this hill country that the LORD promised me that day" (Josh. 14:10–12). Joshua gave Hebron to Caleb along with a blessing. "Then the land had rest from war" (v. 15).

Sometimes we wait a lifetime for a blessing from the LORD. We must believe wholeheartedly like Caleb and lead people who are watching us to never give up despite challenges. The Lord is always faithful to his promises if we are faithful to him. We must not discourage others with faithlessness; it could lead them down a destructive path. We have a responsibility to God, to ourselves, and to others to believe God. When we waver, we must remember God's faithfulness to his promises in the past to help us remain faithful in our future.

There is another land that has been promised for believers—our heavenly home. Sure, there are obstacles, but God has promised heaven to us if we believe. Many leaders will fall into disbelief, and many of their followers will "band together" and also disbelieve, prompting even more people to disbelieve.

Remember the faith of Caleb—with God, you can "swallow up" any obstacle that deters you from believing His promises, and **"We can certainly do it!"**

There are men and women throughout the Bible whose courage impacted the lives of many around them. You never know when you will be used to change the life of another. Having courage amid a storm in your life is one of the most impactful ways you can display your courage.

1. Reflect on the story of Caleb, "When One Man Believes." How does his courage inspire you?

_____
_____
_____
_____
_____
_____
_____
_____
_____
_____
_____
_____

Caleb has similar courage to a man in the New Testament. In the *Beauty Beyond the Thorns* book, you will read about how a man with a shriveled hand had courage to show his weakness to all around him. Those who watched him obey Jesus to hold out his hand instead of running away were deeply impacted. They learned a form of courage we often forget exists—vulnerability.

When we are vulnerable, not hiding behind our weakness, God can use our vulnerability to help others find courage themselves.

Q: *"Being open about your weaknesses is a courageous act to be emulated."*
– Darci J. Steiner

2. I want to hold out my weakness for God to use in the way of his choosing. Will you hold out yours too, like the man with the shriveled hand did? What does this look like for you?

3. Write your weaknesses below. God can turn these into strengths. Don't feel discouraged.

4. Do you hide them, or do you talk with others about them?

5. Have you tried to be courageous by being vulnerable?

6. Have you held out your weaknesses courageously for God to use in a way of his choosing?

Vulnerability breeds vulnerability.

If you are vulnerable with others, they will likely be vulnerable with you.

7. How has being vulnerable made an impact on those around you?

8. Give it a try with someone who is trustworthy. Hold out your hand, your weakness, for God to use to make it into something useful, beautiful, and impactful.

Chapter 8 – The Gift of Joy

Unleashed Gratitude

"How can we know what joy is without having suffered?"

Read chapter 8 of *Beauty Beyond the Thorns*.

"How can we know what joy is without having suffered?" That's right. Read that again. It's a paradox. If we never suffer, we would never be able to feel or understand joy. Even in suffering we can be joyful if we surrender and trust God through our trial.

I have been disabled, hardly able to bear weight, for three years. Not only am I limited, but I have severe pain daily, constantly.

This pain has been a *gift*. This pain has unbound my expression of joy to God. I won't give away the story I tell in chapter 8 of the book, but God has taught me about joy through my suffering.

1. Have you experienced joy in your suffering or in hindsight of what you have suffered? If so, write a thank you note to God.

   _____
   _____
   _____
   _____
   _____
   _____
   _____

2. If you *have not* found joy in your suffering, how do you reason finding joy could even be possible? Write a note to God asking him to help you discover joy.

   _____
   _____
   _____

_____
_____
_____
_____
_____

My disability has created space for a dream to come true—the writing of *Beauty Beyond the Thorns: Discovering Gifts in Suffering* AND this study guide! If it weren't for my disability, I don't believe my dream of writing a book would have become a reality.

You see, I was a perfectionist. Perfectionism stunts growth and creativity. Now I'm grateful for my dis-*abilities* and want God to use my imperfect self to help other imperfect people.

God created space in me through my disability for him to move.

He may be doing the same for you through

your suffering.

Chapter 9 – The Gift of Community

Air Pocket

"How can we know what community is until we make space for others?"

Read chapter 9 of *Beauty Beyond the Thorns*.

Autonomous. Independent. Maverick.

Do these words describe you? I used to strive for these qualities, until I realized I needed help. I can't do everything on my own, and neither can you, no matter how much of a maverick you think you are.

We were made for community—to have friends. If we are going to have friends, we must make space for them. Yes, we do also need to have boundaries and not exhaust ourselves by having too many friends.

Before my injury, I was at a place where I didn't have many friends outside of family. I was very independent, working, and happy to be alone or with family.

I had been hurt by friends who left our friendship without explaining why, friends who moved, and people who I tried to befriend but didn't reciprocate.

When I got hurt at the wedding, I hated that I now needed help beyond family and didn't have a community of deep friends. I had neglected to build them over the years.

There will come a time for you when you need deep friendships. If you don't have a tribe, a friendship group, a Bible study, a support system, go find one. You may not need them now, but *what if they need you?*

1. Where can you find a healthy, life-giving tribe? Write down three ideas, or people, then pray for direction. Take away your excuses and go find your tribe! You weren't made to be fully autonomous.

    ➢

    ➢

    ➢

K.J. Ramsey, in *This too Shall Last*, writes…

Q: *"If our Savior chose to enter the human story in a human body, then we should enter one another's places of suffering remembering we carry and extend the presence of Christ."* – K.J. Ramsey[2]

You may not think you have time, but when you have a need, and someone chooses to enter your suffering, don't you feel the presence of Christ? Whose life can you enter with a gift of your presence? You are being like Christ to them.

1. Who around you is suffering?

   _____

   _____

   _____

2. How can you enter their story to emulate Christ? Be specific and make a plan.

   _____

   _____

   _____

   _____

   _____

   _____

   _____

   _____

Chapter 10 – The Gift of Transformation

A Caregiver's Perspective

Based on Mark Steiner's Chapter

*"How can we be formed without carving and chiseling?
He is forming us into who he intends us to be."*

Read chapter 10 of *Beauty Beyond the Thorns.*

Caregivers need care.

Their needs are often neglected.

My husband Mark helps me with tasks I can't do for myself. He rearranges his schedule to accommodate my needs. He cooks, cleans, and does everything that requires driving or walking. It is a heavy load. Many of you are in the same position. Your load is wearing you down. It's important to ask for and accept help so you don't burn out.

If you *aren't* in this situation, would you be willing to lighten a caregiver's load?

You may think, "I don't have time," but neither does the caregiver. The caregiver has no choice.

1. Would you consider offering to pick up a few items from the store for them when you go for your family? Or stop by with a card or meal? Just do it.

Please do not say to someone in need, "Let me know if I can help you."
Trust me, they won't. It's too awkward!

Instead, if you call and say, "Hey, I'm bringing you dinner this week, which night would work best for you?" then they will gratefully accept your help.

Things you can offer to do for a caregiver:

- ➢ Say something to them so they feel noticed. "Hey, I see how you care for your wife, and I think you are amazing!"
- ➢ Encourage them with a small gift, like a cup of coffee, or a bagel.
- ➢ Take them out for an evening so they can enjoy time away from their situation. Make sure and have someone take their place for the person they care for.
- ➢ Mow their lawn, rake leaves, pull weeds, trim dead branches/trees, other yardwork.
- ➢ Shovel their walk, walk their dog, wash their car, run an errand.
- ➢ Make a meal, not excluding a healthy breakfast. (A friend of ours brought yogurt and toppings for a yogurt bar. I will never forget it.)
- ➢ Clean their home or give them a gift certificate to have it done professionally.
- ➢ Call and leave a message of encouragement without an expectation they'll call you back. They have a difficult time keeping up with all their tasks.

2. Are you willing to be an advocate for a caregiver? Caregivers need help even if they act like they are in control. Approach them (or their advocate) in private and offer specific thought-out help.

A note to caregivers: Is there someone you can ask to be an advocate for you, whom you can communicate your needs to, and who can then organize help for you and the person you are caring for? When you have someone advocating for you, it's much easier to accept help and less awkward for both sides.

If you are a caregiver, remember what you are going through is not to be blamed on whom you are caring for. God has allowed this adversity in your life to help form you. It is your trial together with whom you are caring for. You, the one you are caring for, and God are all on the same team.

If you feel you are being held back because of the person you are caring for, remember God is forming YOU for his purpose, and his purpose is always good and perfect.

Chapter 11 – The Gift of Faith

A Meteorologist's Faith

"How can we know how to have faith without learning from others who embody it?"

Read chapter 11 of *Beauty Beyond the Thorns*.

1. In the story below (Matt. 8:5–13), underline the words of the centurion.

The Faith of the Centurion

> When Jesus had entered Capernaum, a centurion came to him, asking for help. "Lord," he said, "my servant lies at home paralyzed, suffering terribly."

Jesus said to him, "Shall I come and heal him?"

The centurion replied, "Lord, I do not deserve to have you come under my roof. But just say the word, and my servant will be healed. For I myself am a man under authority, with soldiers under me. I tell this one, 'Go,' and he goes; and that one, 'Come,' and he comes. I say to my servant, 'Do this,' and he does it."

When Jesus heard this, he was amazed and said to those following him, "Truly I tell you, I have not found anyone in Israel with such great faith. I say to you that many will come from the east and the west, and will take their places at the feast with Abraham, Isaac and Jacob in the kingdom of heaven. But the subjects of the kingdom will be thrown outside, into the darkness, where there will be weeping and gnashing of teeth."

Then Jesus said to the centurion, "Go! Let it be done just as you believed it would." And his servant was healed at that moment.

2. What is the first word he said to Jesus? _____

3. What does this tell you about him? Discuss this with your group, or if you are studying alone, ponder his situation.

_____

_____

4. The centurion was a Roman. Romans *killed* Romans who believed in Jesus! Did he approach Jesus about something for himself?

5. Do you think he had any needs for himself he could have asked Jesus for?

6. Do you ask Jesus to help those around you in need, or are your prayers focused more on desires for yourself?

7. Notice what Jesus' first words were to the man. Why do you think Jesus asked him this question?

8. Notice the centurion's reply. What was the first word of this sentence?

Notice the humility of his entire response. Even though he was a leader of 100 soldiers, he was humble. True leaders embrace humility, not arrogance, or narcissism.

And what does humility precede? Great faith!

Notice further in the section you have already underlined. "… just say the word, and my servant will be healed." These words exemplified the purest faith Jesus had witnessed in Israel! Jesus said, "Truly I tell you, I have not found anyone in Israel with such great faith."

9. Who heard Jesus say these words besides the centurion? _____

Those who witnessed the faith of the centurion were blessed with a gift—an example of faith. And what did the centurion receive? A healed servant. His servant was obviously valuable to him, also showing the humility he embodied.

10. Who around you embodies great faith?

_____
_____
_____
_____

11. What have you learned from them?

_____
_____
_____
_____
_____
_____
_____
_____

12. Can you spend more time with them? We become like people we spend time with!

Chapter 12 – The Gift of Mercy

Mr. Miyagi

"How can we know what mercy is until we've practiced gifting it?"

Read chapter 12 of *Beauty Beyond the Thorns*.

If you are alone, or in a group, plan ahead to watch the movie *Karate Kid Part II*. Pay close attention to the character, Mr. Miyagi, throughout.

1. In your own words, define mercy.

   _____
   _____
   _____

2. Read Matthew 5:7 and write it here:

   _____
   _____

3. Now, write Matthew 5:7 again, this time replacing "mercy" with some of the words you wrote above.

   _____
   _____
   _____
   _____
   _____

4. Who comes to mind that needs mercy extended to them? Are you willing?

   _____
   _____
   _____

Chapter 13 – The Gift of Repentance

Walking Toward the Cross

"How can we know what repentance is until we walk toward the cross instead of a comfortable life?"

Read chapter 13 of *Beauty Beyond the Thorns*.

How is repentance a gift? Because to repent we need God's help, and his help is a gift!

1. In the center of sin is self. In the center of the cross is God. To repent, we need to lay our sins down at the foot of the cross. Read the section in *Beauty Beyond the Thorns* named "Matthew." What do you think it was like for Matthew to go from being a wealthy tax collector to following a homeless man?

2. How do you think his repentance affected those around him who were watching him repent, walking toward God instead of a comfortable life?

3. Our repentance not only changes us, but also those who are watching us. What are you currently repenting of? Repentance is recurring. We always need to be repenting of something!

Turn around and walk toward the cross instead of a comfortable, selfish lifestyle. Repentance is an act of love toward God.

4. Read Matthew 25:31–46. Underline what speaks to you.

The Sheep and the Goats

> "When the Son of Man comes in his glory, and all the angels with him, he will sit on his glorious throne. All the nations will be gathered before him, and he will separate the people one from another as a shepherd separates the sheep from the goats. He will put the sheep on his right and the goats on his left.

"Then the King will say to those on his right, 'Come, you who are blessed by my Father; take your inheritance, the kingdom prepared for you since the creation of the world. For I was hungry and you gave me something to eat, I was thirsty and you gave me something to drink, I was a stranger and you invited me in, I needed clothes and you clothed me, I was sick and you looked after me, I was in prison and you came to visit me.'

"Then the righteous will answer him, 'Lord, when did we see you hungry and feed you, or thirsty and give you something to drink? When did we see you a stranger and invite you in, or needing clothes and clothe you? When did we see you sick or in prison and go to visit you?'

"The King will reply, 'Truly I tell you, whatever you did for one of the least of these brothers and sisters of mine, you did for me.'

"Then he will say to those on his left, 'Depart from me, you who are cursed, into the eternal fire prepared for the devil and his angels. For I was hungry and you gave me nothing to eat, I was thirsty and you gave me nothing to drink, I was a stranger and you did not invite me in, I needed clothes and you did not clothe me, I was sick and in prison and you did not look after me.'

"They also will answer, 'Lord, when did we see you hungry or thirsty or a stranger or needing clothes or sick or in prison, and did not help you?'

"He will reply, 'Truly I tell you, whatever you did not do for one of the least of these, you did not do for me.'

"Then they will go away to eternal punishment, but the righteous to eternal life" (Matt. 25:31–46).

Who is the author of the passage? Matthew is! The former tax collector who scammed people of their money! He was used by God to write one of the four Gospels! God will use you also. Go to him now and repent. He loves you.

Chapter 14 – The Gift of Endurance

Purer Than Gold

"How can we know what endurance is without being refined by fire?"

Read chapter 14 of *Beauty Beyond the Thorns*.

1. If you were an Olympian, which medal would you prefer—gold, silver, or bronze?

Gold is a precious metal, and to an Olympian a *precious* medal. Gold medalists feel the heat when they repeatedly practice the tiniest incremental movements of their sport, and their muscles burn.

Gold is purified by heating at high temperatures to separate the impurities (dross) from the pure metal. The impurities rise to the top and are skimmed off.

2. What fire have you been enduring?

_____
_____
_____
_____
_____

> ➤ Does it seem to last and last? While fire burns, it purifies. You don't know how your particular fire is purifying you, but believing it is is an act of faith. Instead of being angry with God, can you trust that the purification he is allowing you will lead to something good? That takes a lot of faith, doesn't it? Write how this makes you feel.

> ➤ You might be saying, "But you don't know what I'm going through." I don't. **But God sees you, and he knows how difficult it is.** You may never know the "why"

to your suffering. Job didn't, even though he and God actually spoke about his suffering! And look how Job's story has impacted the world!

Your story is making an impact too.

Keep enduring. If you go to God daily, reading his Word and praying, you will make it through, day by day. This is endurance!

He is working something great in you!

Q: *"Enduring suffering can become a gift because it is an opportunity for us to grow from who we are into who God intends for us to become. He uses suffering to form us."*

– Darci J. Steiner

3. Read the passage below. Discuss with your group how to throw off hinderances and sins that entangle. Underline the words that come before "… he endured the cross.…" How can we endure our cross? Now underline the last sentence in the passage. How does his endurance help ours?

   ➤ Therefore, since we are surrounded by such a great cloud of witnesses, let us throw off everything that hinders and the sin that so easily entangles. And let us run with perseverance the race marked out for us, fixing our eyes on Jesus, the pioneer and perfecter of faith. For the joy set before him he endured the cross, scorning its shame, and sat down at the right hand of the throne of God. Consider him who **endured** such opposition from sinners, so that you will not grow weary and lose heart (Heb. 12:1–3).

   _____
   _____
   _____
   _____

Chapter 15 – The Gift of Direction

Dirt Roads

"How can we know what direction to go when we do not have control of our steps? Our paths get thwarted, but from God's perspective, our path always points to him—True North."

Read chapter 15 of *Beauty Beyond the Thorns.*

Look at the section in Chapter 15, "Vengeance."

1. Have you ever felt or acted as I did when I tried to teach the teenager a lesson? What was your circumstance? How could you have handled it differently if you had followed the verse below?

> ➢ It is mine to avenge; I will repay (Deut. 32:35).

> ➢ Write this verse on a 3x5 card and memorize it. Keep it in your heart for next time you want to give "an eye for an eye."

Q: *"Humility is strength that leaves room for God's grace to be sufficient."*
– Darci J Steiner

Chapter 16 – The Gift of Fulfillment

Food and Addictions Do Not Fulfill

"How can we know what fulfillment is until we let God alone fill?"

Read Chapter 16 of *Beauty Beyond the Thorns*.

Look at the section, "Tricky, Tricky."

1. Can you think of any natural foods (foods God made) that are salty, sugary, *and* high in fat? If so, write them here. There are few to none.

2. What are your thoughts about control being the reason we undereat, possibly leading to anorexia, or the lack of control many of us have in overeating, possibly leading to overweight/obesity?

> Food and other addictions will not fulfill us—only God can fulfill.

As a nutrition counselor, working with clients over the past 15 years, I've realized how often people seek nutrition counseling because food isn't fulfilling them. There is something different they crave. In my observation, if they don't know Jesus, the struggle is more difficult. Food and other addictions never fulfill. God created us with a desire to know *him*.

> ➢ From one man he made all the nations, that they should inhabit the whole earth; and he marked out their appointed times in history and the boundaries of their lands. God did this **so that** they would seek him and perhaps reach out for him and find him, though he is not far from any one of us (Acts 17:26–27).

> ➢ He has made everything beautiful in its time. He has also **set eternity in the human heart**; yet no one can fathom what God has done from beginning to end (Ecc. 3:11).

If we try to stuff the absence of him in our lives with anything but him. We will never truly find lasting fulfillment. Read Daniel 1:8.

> ➤ But Daniel resolved not to defile himself with the royal food and wine, and he asked the chief official for permission not to defile himself this way (Dan 1:8).

3. What do you think "royal" food included?

4. What foods are "royal" to you?

If desserts and snacks are replacing meals, and if you can't stop cravings for salty, sugary, and fatty foods, do what Daniel did and avoid them altogether.

Name three unhealthy foods you may be addicted to.

    1.

    2.

    3.

Choose not to defile yourself and begin a plan to wean from them. You don't have to be stuck in food addiction. You can recover just like other addicts can. It is a battle, I've been there, but you can overcome. It won't happen overnight, *but it won't happen at all if you never begin.*

If you are stuck in other addictions, the same principles apply. Do you struggle with other addictions such as pornography, drugs or alcohol, gambling, lust, stealing, lying, sex, cutting, video games, shopping, working, exercising, etc.?

Read all of Romans chapter 8 below. <u>Underline</u> whatever words fill you with *hope!*

Life Through the Spirit

> Therefore, there is now no condemnation for those who are in Christ Jesus, because through Christ Jesus the law of the Spirit who gives life has set you free from the law of sin and death. For what the law was powerless to do because it was weakened by the flesh, God did by sending his own Son in the likeness of sinful flesh to be a sin offering. And so he condemned sin in the flesh, in order that the righteous requirement of the law might be fully met in us, who do not live according to the flesh but according to the Spirit.

Those who live according to the flesh have their minds set on what the flesh desires; but those who live in accordance with the Spirit have their minds set on what the Spirit desires. The mind governed by the flesh is death, but the mind governed by the Spirit is life and peace. The mind governed by the flesh is hostile to God; it does not submit to God's law, nor can it do so. Those who are in the realm of the flesh cannot please God.

You, however, are not in the realm of the flesh but are in the realm of the Spirit, if indeed the Spirit of God lives in you. And if anyone does not have the Spirit of Christ, they do not belong to Christ. But if Christ is in you, then even though your body is subject to death because of sin, the Spirit gives life because of righteousness. And if the Spirit of him who raised Jesus from the dead is living in you, he who raised Christ from the dead will also give life to your mortal bodies because of his Spirit who lives in you.

Therefore, brothers and sisters, we have an obligation—but it is not to the flesh, to live according to it. For if you live according to the flesh, you will die; but if by the Spirit you put to death the misdeeds of the body, you will live.

For those who are led by the Spirit of God are the children of God. The Spirit you received does not make you slaves, so that you live in fear again; rather, the Spirit you received brought about your adoption to sonship. And by him we cry, *"Abba, Father."* The Spirit himself testifies with our spirit that we are God's children. Now if we are children, then we are heirs—heirs of God and co-heirs with Christ, if indeed we share in his sufferings in order that we may also share in his glory.

Present Suffering and Future Glory

I consider that our present sufferings are not worth comparing with the glory that will be revealed in us. For the creation waits in eager expectation for the children of God to be revealed. For the creation was subjected to frustration, not by its own choice, but by the will of the one who subjected it, in hope that the creation itself will be liberated from its bondage to decay and brought into the freedom and glory of the children of God.

We know that the whole creation has been groaning as in the pains of childbirth right up to the present time. Not only so, but we ourselves, who have the first fruits of the Spirit, groan inwardly as we wait eagerly for our adoption to sonship, the redemption of our bodies. For in this hope we were saved. But hope that is seen is no hope at all. Who hopes for what they already have? But if we hope for what we do not yet have, we wait for it patiently.

In the same way, the Spirit helps us in our weakness. We do not know what we ought to pray for, but the Spirit himself intercedes for us through wordless groans. And he who searches our hearts knows the mind of the Spirit, because the Spirit intercedes for God's people in accordance with the will of God.

And we know that in all things God works for the good of those who love him, who have been called according to his purpose. For those God foreknew he also predestined to be conformed to the image of his Son, that he might be the firstborn among many brothers and sisters. And those he predestined, he also called; those he called, he also justified; those he justified, he also glorified.

More Than Conquerors

What, then, shall we say in response to these things? If God is for us, who can be against us? He who did not spare his own Son, but gave him up for us all—how will he not also, along with him, graciously give us all things? Who will bring any charge against those whom God has chosen? It is God who justifies. Who then is the one who condemns? No one. Christ Jesus who died—more than that, who was raised to life—is at the right hand of God and is also interceding for us. Who shall separate us from the love of Christ? Shall trouble or hardship or persecution or famine or nakedness or danger or sword? As it is written:

"For your sake we face death all day long;
   we are considered as sheep to be slaughtered."

No, in all these things we are more than conquerors through him who loved us. For I am convinced that neither death nor life, neither angels nor demons, neither the present nor the future, nor any powers, neither height nor depth, nor anything else in all creation, will be able to separate us from the love of God that is in Christ Jesus our Lord.

Chapter 17 – The Gift of Provision

Exponential Multiplication

"How can we not know what provision is when God made creation to recreate fish, fowl, beasts, plants, and trees?"

Read chapter 17 of *Beauty Beyond the Thorns*.

Do you know the difference between the feeding of the 5000+ and the 4000+ people? 1,000 people!

Seriously, the 5000+ crowd was *Jewish*, and the 4000+ crowd was *Gentile*.

God fed and healed *both* Jews and Gentiles.

We forget that God still creates seed-bearing plants, fruit-bearing trees, fish in the waters, and beasts on land. He multiplies food sources for us daily. We witness miracles every day when we see food on our plate. *We think we did that*—that we brought home the bacon with our paycheck!

But God did that! He is the one who has provided for us.

That is why we should say thank you when we eat.

Like the disciples and crowds were shown how God multiplied a little boy's lunch, we too are given the task to provide "a lunch" for God to multiply.

When we give financially, or otherwise, God can multiply our gifts. God provides us with resources, and he will multiply our efforts, but we must first take the step of giving before he can multiply.

1. In what ways do you help feed people who are hungry?

2. Do you give a little for God to multiply?

3. Who needs a hand around you? If you can't give much, it's okay; give a little bit and God will use it in ways you may never see. That's part of the fun of giving!

4. Give someone "a lunch" today for God to multiply. Who is God bringing to mind?

   _____

Chapter 18 – The Gift of a Shepherd

Jesus Rescues Cast Sheep

*"How can we understand the gift of our shepherd
if we don't understand the needs of a sheep?"*

Read chapter 18 of *Beauty Beyond the Thorns*.

1. Read Luke 13:10–17 below.

   ### Jesus Heals a Crippled Woman on the Sabbath

   > On a Sabbath Jesus was teaching in one of the synagogues, and a woman was there who had been crippled by a spirit for eighteen years. She was bent over and could not straighten up at all. When Jesus saw her, he called her forward and said to her, "Woman, you are set free from your infirmity." Then he put his hands on her, and immediately she straightened up and praised God.
   >
   > Indignant because Jesus had healed on the Sabbath, the synagogue leader said to the people, "There are six days for work. So come and be healed on those days, not on the Sabbath."
   >
   > The Lord answered him, "You hypocrites! Doesn't each of you on the Sabbath untie your ox or donkey from the stall and lead it out to give it water? Then should not this woman, a daughter of Abraham, whom Satan has kept bound for eighteen long years, be set free on the Sabbath day from what bound her?"
   >
   > When he said this, all his opponents were humiliated, but the people were delighted with all the wonderful things he was doing.

2. What did the crippled woman do after Jesus straightened her back?

3. What did the synagogue ruler do?

4. What was the difference between the synagogue ruler's response to the woman versus Jesus' response?

5. All of us are bent double in some way—in need of some change. If you audibly heard Jesus' voice call you forward, how would you feel? What would you do?

6. He calls us to come to him daily. How does that make you feel? What emoji do you attach to your answer?

7. Name several ways we can *go to* him.

You can listen to the voice of Jesus in the red print in the Gospels.

8. Read Matthew chapter 7:7–12 below. These are the words of Jesus. When you read, imagine walking with Jesus while he teaches you these things.

    ➢ Ask and it will be given to you; seek and you will find; knock and the door will be opened to you. For everyone who asks receives; the one who seeks finds; and to the one who knocks, the door will be opened.

    Which of you, if your son asks for bread, will give him a stone? Or if he asks for a fish, will give him a snake? If you, then, though you are evil, know how to give good gifts to your children, how much more will your Father in heaven give good gifts to those who ask him! So in everything, do to others what you would have them do to you, for this sums up the Law and the Prophets.

9. What do you hear him saying?

   _____
   _____
   _____
   _____

10. Read Psalm 23, written for you below. Circle all the words that refer to God.

   ➢ **A Psalm of David**

   The LORD is my shepherd, I lack nothing.
      He makes me lie down in green pastures,
   he leads me beside quiet waters,
      he refreshes my soul.
   He guides me along the right paths
      for his name's sake.
   Even though I walk
      through the darkest valley,
   I will fear no evil,
      for you are with me;
   your rod and your staff,
      they comfort me.

   You prepare a table before me
      in the presence of my enemies.
   You anoint my head with oil;
      my cup overflows.
   Surely your goodness and love will follow me
      all the days of my life,
   and I will dwell in the house of the LORD
      forever.

Chapter 19 – The Gift of Touch

Lepers

"How can we understand the value of touch if we've never held the hand of a sufferer?"

Read chapter 19 of *Beauty Beyond the Thorns*.

1. Have you ever seen a leper? What was your experience?

2. Even if you haven't seen one, how do you think you'd respond if you did?

3. Talk or think about why Jesus *touched* lepers to heal them. Did he *have* to? Or did he *choose* to?

4. Who are some metaphorical lepers around you (hint: the elderly) that could use a healthy touch from you? A backrub, a handheld, a high five, a handshake, a hug.

5. Read the full story of Naaman in your Bible, 2 Kings 5. Read the section in the book "God Cannot Be Bought." What does this phrase mean?

_____

_____

6. Gehazi, a servant of Elisha, felt Naaman should have given Elisha something for healing him. When Elisha refused, what do you think Gehazi felt?

_____
_____
_____

7. Why do you suppose he lied to Naaman? Are you tempted to feel you are owed something when you do something nice for someone? Or do you give with no strings attached?

Unconditional love gives with no strings attached.

8. Naaman had in mind how he thought his healing should occur. Name three examples of how you have struggled to do things the way God wants instead of the way *you* think things should happen.

   ➢

   ➢

   ➢

9. Gehazi's greed and deceitfulness earned him the high-priced consequence of leprosy. How serious do you think God is when he sees us being greedy and deceitful?

10. How can you repent of greed?

_____
_____
_____

11. How can you repent of deceitfulness? Do you exaggerate? Alter a detail?

_____

_____

_____

Jesus physically touched the lives of many people while he walked the earth. Here are some examples:

> ➢ Jesus reached out his hand and **touch**ed the man. "I am willing," he said. "Be clean!" Immediately he was cleansed of his leprosy (Matt. 8:3).

> ➢ He **touch**ed her hand and the fever left her, and she got up and began to wait on him (Matt. 8:15).

> ➢ Just then a woman who had been subject to bleeding for twelve years came up behind him and **touch**ed the edge of his cloak. She said to herself, "If I only **touch** his cloak, I will be healed" (Matt. 9:20–21).

> ➢ Then he **touch**ed their eyes and said, "According to your faith let it be done to you" (Matt. 9:29).

> ➢ … and begged him to let the sick just **touch** the edge of his cloak, and all who **touch**ed it were healed (Matt. 14:36).

> ➢ But Jesus came and **touch**ed them. "Get up," he said. "Don't be afraid" (Matt. 17:7).

> ➢ Jesus had compassion on them and **touch**ed their eyes. Immediately they received their sight and followed him (Matt. 20:34).

Chapter 20 – The Gift of Gratitude

One Leper

"If we don't express gratitude, is it because we feel entitled?"

Read chapter 20 of *Beauty Beyond the Thorns*.

1. Make a list of all the good things God has done for you today, including protecting you from bad things that *have not* happened to you. Dig deep.

   _____
   _____
   _____

2. Have you expressed your gratitude to him yet for each of these things?

Get in the practice of thanking God throughout the day—for the things he does for you. He doesn't owe us anything. Let's not take him for granted.

3. Circle in the book all the ways the grateful leper expressed his appreciation to Jesus for healing him.

4. Read the verse below and circle all the things God does for you.

   ➢ Praise the LORD, my soul,
       and forget not all his benefits—
   who forgives all your sins
       and heals all your diseases,
   who redeems your life from the pit
       and crowns you with love and compassion,

>   who satisfies your desires with good things
>   so that your youth is renewed like the eagle's (Ps. 103:2–5).

5. Write a prayer to God below in gratitude for loving you in the ways described in Psalm 103.

   Dear God,

   _____
   _____
   _____
   _____
   _____

6. What do you imagine he would write to you in return?

   Dear (your name),

   _____
   _____
   _____
   _____
   _____

7. Who or what in your life have you been taking for granted? How can you change this?

   _____
   _____
   _____
   _____

Chapter 21 – The Gift of a Good Samaritan

Inconvenient Love

"How can we know how to be a good Samaritan if we don't allow ourselves to be inconvenienced to help someone in need?"

Read chapter 21 of *Beauty Beyond the Thorns*.

1. Read the following story from the Bible.

The Parable of the Good Samaritan

> On one occasion an expert in the law stood up to test Jesus. "Teacher," he asked, "what must I do to inherit eternal life?"

"What is written in the Law?" he replied. "How do you read it?"

He answered, "'Love the Lord your God with all your heart and with all your soul and with all your strength and with all your mind'; and, 'Love your neighbor as yourself.'"

"You have answered correctly," Jesus replied. "Do this and you will live."

But he wanted to justify himself, so he asked Jesus, "And who is my neighbor?"

In reply Jesus said: "A man was going down from Jerusalem to Jericho, when he was attacked by robbers. They stripped him of his clothes, beat him and went away, leaving him half dead. A priest happened to be going down the same road, and when he saw the man, he passed by on the other side. So too, a Levite, when he came to the place and saw him, passed by on the other side. But a Samaritan, as he traveled, came where the man was; and when he saw him, he took pity on him. He went to him and bandaged his wounds, pouring on oil and wine. Then he put the man on his own donkey, brought him to an inn and took care of him. The next day he took out two denarii and gave them to the innkeeper. 'Look after him,' he said, 'and when I return, I will reimburse you for any extra expense you may have.'

"Which of these three do you think was a neighbor to the man who fell into the hands of robbers?"

The expert in the law replied, "The one who had mercy on him."

Jesus told him, "Go and do likewise" (Luke 10:25–37).

2. Write a story about someone in your life who has come to your rescue like the *Good Samaritan* did for the man who fell into the hands of the robbers.

   _____
   _____
   _____
   _____
   _____
   _____

3. Write a story of how you can be a *Good Samaritan* for someone; serving them even though it is inconvenient for you.

   _____
   _____
   _____
   _____
   _____
   _____

You may never know the impact you make, but they know, and God knows. No one else needs to know.

This is love.

Chapter 22 – The Gift of Forgiveness

A Thirty-Year Prayer

*"How can we know what forgiveness is until
we have been utterly broken by our sin?"*

Read chapter 22 of *Beauty Beyond the Thorns*.

If you are having difficulties in your relationship with someone, it may be because you don't know their full story: why they are the way they are. They have a history you may not know about. I didn't know about my dad's childhood trauma, but when he opened up about it, a lot of things came together for me and my perspective of him changed. If you can have an open conversation with someone where both parties share about the difficulties you have each endured, it may help both of you move forward in the relationship.

If this is not possible, try to extend grace, knowing you may not know everything that person has endured. We are the way we are, in part, because of trauma or suffering we have endured.

We have hurt people too. We need to be forgiven *as much* as we need to forgive.

1. Read the following passages, then write what speaks to you below.

    ➢ Be kind and compassionate to one another, forgiving each other, just as in Christ God forgave you (Eph. 4:32).

    ➢ Be merciful, just as your Father is merciful. Do not judge, and you will not be judged. Do not condemn, and you will not be condemned. Forgive, and you will be forgiven. Give, and it will be given to you. A good measure, pressed down, shaken together and running over, will be poured into your lap. For with the measure you use, it will be measured to you (Luke 6:36–38).

> Do not judge, or you too will be judged. For in the same way you judge others, you will be judged, and with the measure you use, it will be measured to you. Why do you look at the speck of sawdust in your brother's eye and pay no attention to the plank in your own eye? How can you say to your brother, "Let me take the speck out of your eye," when all the time there is a plank in your own eye? You hypocrite, first take the plank out of your own eye, and then you will see clearly to remove the speck from your brother's eye (Matt. 7:1–5).

2. Recently, I've noticed many relationships have been severed due to political differences. We currently live in a "cancel culture" where if we don't like something, we just erase it from our lives. How can we just cancel people out of our lives?

    Yes, there are dangerous relationships this concept does not apply to. But if you are having differences in non-dangerous relationships, a better way to work through differences is by talking, not just erasing people because you disagree with their views.

    Canceling people from our lives creates grave pain for both parties, whether you know it or not.

    If you are in a situation like this, would you consider having a conversation(s) with this/these person/people? In person if possible.

    I was ready to walk away from my dad, but when I leaned into the pain and learned about him, we both were able to heal beyond our wildest dreams! I learned to *love* Dad, when for a lot of my life I hated him.

3. Pray together in a group, or by yourself, for healing in difficult relationships. Ask God to guide you and for his Spirit to move your relationship in a direction of healing.

Chapter 23 – The Gift of Sight

The God Who Sees

"How can we know what sight is without following the One who sees?"

Read chapter 23 of *Beauty Beyond the Thorns*.

1. Read these verses about how God sees us:

   ➢ Does he who formed the **eye** not **see**? (Ps. 94:9).

   ➢ From heaven the Lord **looks** down and **sees** all mankind; from his dwelling place he **watches** all who live on earth (Ps. 33:13).

   ➢ For the **eyes** of the Lord range throughout the earth to strengthen those whose hearts are fully committed to him (2 Chron. 16:9).

   ➢ My help comes from the Lord, the Maker of heaven and earth. He will not let your foot slip–he who **watches** over you will not slumber; indeed, he who **watches** over Israel will neither slumber nor sleep. The Lord **watches** over you–the Lord is your shade at your right hand; the sun will not harm you by day, nor the moon by night. The Lord will keep you from all harm–he will **watch** over your life; the Lord will **watch** over your coming and going both now and forevermore (Ps. 121:2–8).

2. Look in chapter 23 of the book and write what El Roi means. _____

3. When don't you feel seen by God?

   _____
   _____
   _____
   _____
   _____

4. Reread the section in chapter 23, "God Sees You."

5. Now reread your answers to question #3 and write next to them, "El Roi saw me and was with me." His eyes are always on you and what you are enduring. Don't forget, he is working everything out for your good. He loves you. Be a reflection of him to others, knowing he sees you while you are seeing others.

6. How can you determine to see others better?

   _____
   _____
   _____
   _____

7. Practice seeing, acknowledging, and assisting those around you who may feel unseen. Often it is the elderly or the disabled. Let your compassion allow you to see them through the lens of El Roi. Is someone sitting alone at an event? At church? At a restaurant? Initiate a conversation. How can you let others know they are seen?

   _____
   _____
   _____
   _____

8. Spend some time in prayer thanking God for seeing you, even if you still feel alone. There is no one in the world who sees you better or who knows you better. If you don't see him, you are the one that has to move. He is right there. Pray to know how to draw closer to him so you can also see the One who sees you—El Roi.

Chapter 24 – The Gift of Wholeness

The Only One in the World

Based on Don Talley's Chapter

"How can we be whole if we hide behind our pain?"

Read chapter 24 in *Beauty Beyond the Thorns*.

1. What do you think it feels like to Don Talley that no one else in the world has his disease?

2. Similarly, what in your life makes you feel alone?

3. Do you hate your weakness, your pain, who you are, God? Write about it. If you are willing, share with your group or another person.

4. How can you embrace the things in your life you hate? How can you lean into your pain and face your fears like Don Talley did?

5. How do you think God could use your brokenness to help others? To glorify him? Are you willing? How can you begin?

_____
_____
_____
_____
_____

The Healing at the Pool

➤ Sometime later, Jesus went up to Jerusalem for one of the Jewish festivals. Now there is in Jerusalem near the Sheep Gate a pool, which in Aramaic is called Bethesda and which is surrounded by five covered colonnades. Here a great number of disabled people used to lie—the blind, the lame, the paralyzed. One who was there had been an invalid for thirty-eight years. When Jesus saw him lying there and learned that he had been in this condition for a long time, he asked him, "Do you want to get well?"

"Sir," the invalid replied, "I have no one to help me into the pool when the water is stirred. While I am trying to get in, someone else goes down ahead of me."

Then Jesus said to him, "Get up! Pick up your mat and walk." At once the man was cured; he picked up his mat and walked.

The day on which this took place was a Sabbath, and so the Jewish leaders said to the man who had been healed, "It is the Sabbath; the law forbids you to carry your mat."

But he replied, "The man who made me well said to me, 'Pick up your mat and walk.'"

So they asked him, "Who is this fellow who told you to pick it up and walk?"

The man who was healed had no idea who it was, for Jesus had slipped away into the crowd that was there.

Later Jesus found him at the temple and said to him, "See, you are well again. Stop sinning or something worse may happen to you." The man went away and told the Jewish leaders that it was Jesus who had made him well (John 5:1–15).

6. Are you willing to say, "Yes, I want to be healed," or do you want to continue staying stuck like the invalid at the pool did by making excuses? What excuses are holding you back? Have you ever looked at your situation and thought you were making excuses? If not, this is difficult. It's okay. It's better to realize it now than to stay stuck!

7. Why do you think you've been making excuses? What are you afraid of?

8. Don says, "To be made whole doesn't require physical healing." If you have a physical impairment, you can be made whole on earth before eternal life in heaven. You can be made whole by having a relationship with Jesus Christ. He makes up the difference. If you don't feel ready to go to him, say a prayer and ask him to help you *want to want* him to make you whole.

_____
_____
_____
_____
_____
_____

Chapter 25 – The Gift of Obedience

Learning Obedience Through Suffering

"If Jesus learned obedience through suffering, how will we?"

Read chapter 25 of *Beauty Beyond the Thorns*.

1. Read the story below of Jesus healing a man blind since birth.

Jesus Heals a Man Born Blind

> As he went along, he saw a man blind from birth. His disciples asked him, "Rabbi, who sinned, this man or his parents, that he was born blind?"

"Neither this man nor his parents sinned," said Jesus, "but this happened so that the works of God might be displayed in him. As long as it is day, we must do the works of him who sent me. Night is coming, when no one can work. While I am in the world, I am the light of the world."

After saying this, he spit on the ground, made some mud with the saliva, and put it on the man's eyes. "Go," he told him, "wash in the Pool of Siloam" (this word means "Sent"). So the man went and washed, and came home seeing.

His neighbors and those who had formerly seen him begging asked, "Isn't this the same man who used to sit and beg?" Some claimed that he was.

Others said, "No, he only looks like him."

But he himself insisted, "I am the man."

"How then were your eyes opened?" they asked.

He replied, "The man they call Jesus made some mud and put it on my eyes. He told me to go to Siloam and wash. So I went and washed, and then I could see."

"Where is this man?" they asked him.

"I don't know," he said.

The Pharisees Investigate the Healing

They brought to the Pharisees the man who had been blind. Now the day on which Jesus had made the mud and opened the man's eyes was a Sabbath. Therefore the Pharisees also asked him how he had received his sight. "He put mud on my eyes," the man replied, "and I washed, and now I see."

Some of the Pharisees said, "This man is not from God, for he does not keep the Sabbath."

But others asked, "How can a sinner perform such signs?" So they were divided.

Then they turned again to the blind man, "What have you to say about him? It was your eyes he opened."

The man replied, "He is a prophet."

They still did not believe that he had been blind and had received his sight until they sent for the man's parents. "Is this your son?" they asked. "Is this the one you say was born blind? How is it that now he can see?"

"We know he is our son," the parents answered, "and we know he was born blind. But how he can see now, or who opened his eyes, we don't know. Ask him. He is of age; he will speak for himself." His parents said this because they were afraid of the Jewish leaders, who already had decided that anyone who acknowledged that Jesus was the Messiah would be put out of the synagogue. That was why his parents said, "He is of age; ask him."

A second time they summoned the man who had been blind. "Give glory to God by telling the truth," they said. "We know this man is a sinner."

He replied, "Whether he is a sinner or not, I don't know. One thing I do know. I was blind but now I see!"

Then they asked him, "What did he do to you? How did he open your eyes?"

He answered, "I have told you already and you did not listen. Why do you want to hear it again? Do you want to become his disciples too?"

Then they hurled insults at him and said, "You are this fellow's disciple! We are disciples of Moses! We know that God spoke to Moses, but as for this fellow, we don't even know where he comes from."

The man answered, "Now that is remarkable! You don't know where he comes from, yet he opened my eyes. We know that God does not listen to sinners. He listens to the godly person who does his will. Nobody has ever heard of opening the eyes of a man born blind. If this man were not from God, he could do nothing."

To this they replied, "You were steeped in sin at birth; how dare you lecture us!" And they threw him out.

Spiritual Blindness

Jesus heard that they had thrown him out, and when he found him, he said, "Do you believe in the Son of Man?"

"Who is he, sir?" the man asked. "Tell me so that I may believe in him."

Jesus said, "You have now seen him; in fact, he is the one speaking with you."

Then the man said, "Lord, I believe," and he worshiped him.

Jesus said, "For judgment I have come into this world, so that the blind will see and those who see will become blind."

Some Pharisees who were with him heard him say this and asked, "What? Are we blind too?"

Jesus said, "If you were blind, you would not be guilty of sin; but now that you claim you can see, your guilt remains (John 9:1–41).

2. Wow! Discuss your thoughts or write them below. Write everything you see, hear, and feel.

3. Do you ever find yourself looking for ways *not* to believe in Jesus or his power? When you hear someone speak of Jesus, do you listen to them, or deflect what they are saying, reasoning his miracles couldn't be possible?

4. Count how many times the Pharisees asked the healed man to repeat his story. _____. Did he give them the response they were looking for to disprove Jesus?

5. Read the **Seven Woes on the Teachers of the Law and the Pharisees**

   ➢ **"Woe** to you, teachers of the law and Pharisees, you hypocrites! You shut the door of the kingdom of heaven in people's faces. You yourselves do not enter, nor will you let those enter who are trying to.

   "Woe to you, teachers of the law and Pharisees, you hypocrites! You travel over land and sea to win a single convert, and when you have succeeded, you make them twice as much a child of hell as you are.

   "Woe to you, blind guides! You say, 'If anyone swears by the temple, it means nothing; but anyone who swears by the gold of the temple is bound by that oath.' You blind fools! Which is greater: the gold, or the temple that makes the gold sacred? You also say, 'If anyone swears by the altar, it means nothing; but anyone who swears by the gift on the altar is bound by that oath.' You blind men! Which is greater: the gift, or the altar that makes the gift sacred? Therefore, anyone who swears by the altar swears by it and by everything on it. And anyone who swears by the temple swears by it and by the one who dwells in it. And anyone who swears by heaven swears by God's throne and by the one who sits on it.

   "Woe to you, teachers of the law and Pharisees, you hypocrites! You give a tenth of your spices—mint, dill and cumin. But you have neglected the more important matters of the law—justice, mercy and faithfulness. You should have practiced the latter, without neglecting the former. You blind guides! You strain out a gnat but swallow a camel.

   "Woe to you, teachers of the law and Pharisees, you hypocrites! You clean the outside of the cup and dish, but inside they are full of greed and self-indulgence. Blind Pharisee! First clean the inside of the cup and dish, and then the outside also will be clean.

   "Woe to you, teachers of the law and Pharisees, you hypocrites! You are like whitewashed tombs, which look beautiful on the outside but on the inside are full of the bones of the dead and everything unclean. In the same way, on the outside you appear to people as righteous but on the inside you are full of hypocrisy and wickedness.

   "Woe to you, teachers of the law and Pharisees, you hypocrites! You build tombs for the prophets and decorate the graves of the righteous. And you say, 'If we had lived in the days of our ancestors, we would not have taken part with them in shedding the blood of the prophets.' So you testify against yourselves that you are the descendants of those who murdered the prophets. Go ahead, then, and complete what your ancestors started!" (Matt. 23:13-32).

6. Summarize these "woes" in your own words.

_____

_____

_____

_____

All of us are hypocritical to some point, but the goal is to become less so. I don't want to be like a Pharisee. I want to see like the blind man did when he trusted and obeyed Jesus.

7. Reread the section in chapter 25, "Contrast." Write in the columns below the differences between Jesus and other kings. Hint: How do kings typically live? How did Jesus live his life? I've provided an example in the first column.

Jesus	Kings/Pharisees
Homeless	Palaces

8. Now read **The Beatitudes** in Matthew 5:3–12, provided for you below.

    Blessed are the poor in spirit,
      for theirs is the kingdom of heaven.
    Blessed are those who mourn,
      for they will be comforted.
    Blessed are the meek,
      for they will inherit the earth.
    Blessed are those who hunger and thirst for righteousness,
      for they will be filled.
    Blessed are the merciful,

> for they will be shown mercy.
> Blessed are the pure in heart,
>   for they will see God.
> Blessed are the peacemakers,
>   for they will be called children of God.
> Blessed are those who are persecuted because of righteousness,
>   for theirs is the kingdom of heaven.
> Blessed are you when people insult you, persecute you and falsely say all kinds of evil against you because of me. Rejoice and be glad, because great is your reward in heaven, for in the same way they persecuted the prophets who were before you.

9. In the columns below, write who is blessed in the first column and what they are blessed with in the second column.

Who is blessed?	Blessing?
Poor in spirit	Kingdom of heaven

10. Do you see a theme in the charts of how Jesus is calling people who follow him to live? What do you notice? Are you willing to be meek, poor in spirit, etc.?

This is the revolutionary way Jesus changed the world. We are up against a lifestyle that most of us strive for—more prestige and power. But Jesus wants us to live upside down, backwards, and inside out!

11. How did Jesus learn obedience? _____

12. How do we learn obedience to God? _____

Chapter 26 – The Gift of Light

Good and Evil

"How can we appreciate the light unless we've encountered despairing darkness?"

Read chapter 26 of *Beauty Beyond the Thorns*.

1. Have you ever been in a situation where you felt blind like I did while driving in a storm? What was the circumstance?

   _____
   _____
   _____
   _____

2. When scary things happen to us, we tend to pull back and live in fear. Holocaust survivor Viktor Frankl writes in his book, *Man's Search for Meaning*:

Q: "The prisoner who had lost faith in the future—his future—was doomed. With his loss of belief in the future, he also lost his spiritual hold; he let himself decline and became subject to mental and physical decay."[3] –Viktor Frankl, Man's Search for Meaning

If you have been living in fear, discuss honestly with your group or a friend how you can begin to trust in your future again. How can you take steps to trust again? Look to the light—the light of Jesus in his Word. It's how we can grow in our faith and grow out of fear. Begin reading in the book of John or one of the other Gospels. Get to know Jesus so you don't have to fear your future.

3. Every day we are in a spiritual battle for our souls. Most days we forget because we can't physically see the spiritual realm. Reread the section in the book called "Good and Evil." Write what stands out to you or discuss it with your group.

   _____
   _____
   _____
   _____

4. What original name did God give Satan when he was an angel?

   _____

5. What was Satan's downfall?

   _____

6. Write out Psalm 119:105 and John 8:12 here.

   _____

   _____

   _____

   _____

   _____

   _____

   _____

   _____

   _____

   _____

   _____

Chapter 27 – The Gift of Trust

Job Never Knew the "Why"

"How can we understand trust without living humbly?"

Read chapter 27 of *Beauty Beyond the Thorns*.

1. What was the sin that tripped up Satan, Adam and Eve, and the Pharisees?

2. How can you prevent falling into this same trap?

3. Satan is the father of _____ (John 8:44). How does he lie to you?

4. In Abdu Murray's book, *Saving Truth: Finding Meaning & Clarity in a Post-Truth World*, he says,

Q: "… in wanting to be God instead of being with God—we have become less than our intended and best selves."[4] –Abdu Murray, *Saving Truth: Finding Meaning & Clarity in a Post-Truth World*

Please write or discuss what this quote means to you.

_____
_____
_____
_____
_____

5. Read the section "Job." Please have a great discussion on this section or write your thoughts here.

6. In "Behind the Scenes," what exactly is going on behind the scenes? How does making you aware of this help you?

7. How do we know from Scripture that demons believe in God (Mark 9:25)? If demons believe in God, what does that say about the existence of God? They used to live with him, so of course they recognize him!

_____
_____
_____
_____
_____
_____
_____

Chapter 28 – The Gift of Adoration

Receiving Love

"How can we feel God's love if we don't accept his adoration of us?"

Read chapter 28 of *Beauty Beyond the Thorns*.

1. Do you have a favorite poem or song? What is it? Why do you like it? What does it make you feel or how does it affect you?

   _____
   _____
   _____

2. Have you ever thought about living a poetic life with Jesus and what that would be like? The Greek word for workmanship is _____ which literally means, _____. How does that enhance your understanding of the following verse?

   ➢ "For we are God's workmanship, created in Christ Jesus for good works, which God prepared beforehand, that we should walk in them" (Eph. 2:10, RSV).

   _____
   _____
   _____
   _____

3. For me, understanding the word "poiema" has transformed my relationship with God because it helps me to understand that God wants to live in a poetic relationship with me. It makes me feel adored! Do you have a difficult time feeling adored by God? Does knowing the translation of "workmanship" help you feel closer to God? Write what you feel!

   _____
   _____
   _____

4. Write a poem to God about adoration—giving adoration and receiving adoration. Go ahead, give it a whirl!

5. What helped Joseph get through his years of suffering? Hint: Look at Genesis 50:20.

Chapter 29 – The Gift of Empathy

A Father, a Counselor, and a Big Brother

"How can we understand the empathy of Christ until we grasp that he himself suffered temptation in every way?"

Read chapter 29 of *Beauty Beyond the Thorns*.

1. What is the order of the three main things the Israelites struggled with in their trust of God when they were wandering in the wilderness? Hint: The answer is in the book.

    ➢

    ➢

    ➢

2. What is the order of the three things Satan tempted Jesus with while he was in the wilderness? Hint: The answer is in the book.

    ➢

    ➢

    ➢

3. What prepared Jesus for his ministry? To have empathy? The answer is in the "Temptation" section of the book.

Q: *"Heartache sucks the life out of you unless your life aches for Christ."*
– Darci J. Steiner

4. What does this verse mean to you? "May the God of hope fill you with all joy and peace as you trust in him, so that you may overflow with hope by the power of the Holy Spirit" (Rom. 15:13).

_____
_____
_____
_____
_____

5. What does it feel like when someone is empathetic toward you?

_____
_____
_____
_____
_____

6. How can you grow in your empathy toward others? Remember, using your suffering is a great way to speak into others' sufferings.

_____
_____
_____
_____
_____

Chapter 30 – The Gift of Brokenness

Jesus

"How can we find comfort from God in our brokenness if we don't accept Jesus was pierced for our transgressions?"

Read chapter 30 of *Beauty Beyond the Thorns*.

1. How can brokenness be a gift?

2. Write all the ways you feel broken.

3. Circle the word broke(n), break(s), etc. everywhere you see it written in chapter 30 of *Beauty Beyond the Thorns*.

4. Do you see how Jesus understands brokenness? He has empathy for you because he understands. What are you thinking or feeling?

5. Go to the section, "Why." Reread it to refresh your mind.

6. What is your "why" to help you live with your "how"?

_____
_____
_____
_____
_____
_____
_____

He was pierced for our transgressions.
The punishment that brought us peace was on him.
By his wounds we are healed (Isa. 53:5).

1. Augustine of Hippo, *On Christian Doctrine, Book I*, 27-28
2. K. J. Ramsey and Kelly M. Kapic, *This Too Shall Last: Finding Grace When Suffering Lingers*, (Grand Rapids, MI: Zondervan Reflective, 2020), 39.
3. Viktor E. Frankl, *Man's Search for Meaning*, tr. Ilse Lasch, (Boston: Beacon, 2006), 74.
4. Abdu Murray, *Saving Truth: Finding Meaning & Clarity in a Post-Truth World*, Grand Rapids, MI: Zondervan, 20180, 63.

Quotes from Beauty Beyond the Thorns by ©Darci J. Steiner, Author

"I see beauty beyond the thorns because I see him."

"We want our thorns removed, but the pain from the thorns is the very tool that is healing what most needs to be healed in us—our souls. Satan uses thorns to puncture, but Jesus staunches our wounds with himself."

"Joy and suffering can coexist in the same space; they can be experienced together."

"God may use our suffering [and healing journey] to provide gifts to those around us. When the bleeding woman reached out in faith to touch the fringe of Jesus' cloak, he not only healed her, but—those watching in the crowd found healing for their faithlessness and hopelessness."

"Sometimes, we learn best from our life experiences, but failing to learn lessons from the lives of others, is like staying in a house caught on fire because you've never been burned. You don't have to wait to learn to get out of a burning house until you are stuck in one—you get out because you have learned from other people who haven't been as fortunate."

"It is within suffering that God reveals himself to you just like he revealed himself to the world at the cross. Suffering provides opportunities for you to understand the sufferings of Jesus and draw closer to him. The cross is where darkness and light meet. When you feel you are in the dark, you will find love and hope at the cross."

"Whether your suffering is short or long, he is your refuge from the storm. Jesus—he is the beauty beyond our thorns."

Chapter 1 – The Gift of Hope

"How can we understand hope without having faith?"

"I am learning I can survive my worst fears. Even twice. I am learning to sit in fear and not be afraid because I know God's plans for me are always good. He showed me that before. I believe gifts in suffering are most often given in hindsight so we can grow in trust during its ravages. When I suffer, I am called to a place of discomfort, a place I do not want to be, but a place where God chooses to grow me. It's a place where I must turn around to face him so he can lead in the direction of his choosing. I am not in control. But that's a good thing!"

"Suffering in our lives often doesn't make sense, but God always has a purpose for it, always for our benefit. Jesus dying on the cross didn't make sense, but God had an immense purpose for it—the salvation of our souls. He is our ultimate hope. His plans are better than ours, so we have reason to hope even though we don't understand his allowance of our troubles. Faith is being sure of what we hope for."

"The cross I am carrying, and thorns I bear, are paving the way toward receiving a heavenly crown. 'Blessed is the one who perseveres under trial because, having stood the test, that person will receive the crown of life that the Lord has promised to those who love him'" (James 1:12).

Chapter 2 – The Gift of Perseverance

"How can we know what perseverance is until we've run out of strength?"

"The revolutionary Jesus was in town leading a revolutionary way—those previously considered on top of the religious hierarchy are bump, bump, bumped to the bottom, and those who mourn, the meek, poor in spirit, pure in heart, and those persecuted are now considered great in the kingdom of God."

Chapter 3 – The Gift of Compassion

"How can we know what compassion is until we've emulated it to the degree Jesus exemplified it?"

- "…Jesus wasn't reliant on a person's expression of faith to heal them. He healed people who had faith, and he healed those with no faith."

- "Jesus was more concerned about man than the law, but the Pharisees (religious leaders) were more concerned about the law than man."

- "When we suffer, we are carved, and it hurts. God chisels us through anguish to fulfill the ultimate purpose he has for our lives and even for those around us. Love includes pain because love is the chisel that forms us into who he designed us to be."

Chapter 4 – The Gift of Deliverance

"How can we know what it means to be delivered until we've surrendered?"

- "God uses the people who pray prayers to answer those very prayers."

Chapter 5 – The Gift of Love

"How can we know what love is without allowing ourselves to receive it?"

- "This better-than-a-Hallmark love story is about the Jesus of the Bible, who traded in his crown of thorns to offer us not a small finger ring of gold and diamonds, but instead a heavenly eternal crown."

- "The Bible says God has set eternity in our hearts so that one day we might seek and find him. He made us to want to be in a relationship with him" (See Ecc. 3:11).

Chapter 6 – The Gift of Grace

"How can we understand grace until we've realized our profound need for forgiveness?"

 "Suffering has confirmed for me there is a God, for miracles can only come from him. He has healed pains and solved problems no other being, or icon, could solve."

Chapter 7 – The Gift of Courage

*"How can we know what courage is until we
do something beyond our capabilities?"*

"If we go into hiding, others cannot see God working gloriously through our limitations. God may not choose to heal our physical imperfections during our earthly life, but our hearts can heal, and we can move closer to God the souls of many who are watching us. Like this man [the man with the withered hand], we must courageously choose to obey God and not run away, even when we are afraid. We must have courage to face where we have never been."

 "Pain and imperfections in our lives do not equal a lack of love from God. Instead, they reveal, at the right time, a divine and perfect purpose packed with love."

 "My life is different now, and I am often avoided and looked at and treated as weak. And I was, and am, but at the same time, I'm not. I'm stronger now—more courageous. I am stronger now in many ways than when I could walk. Suffering has taught me not to look at those who are obviously suffering with woeful eyes, but instead to look at them with the utmost respect."

 "I want to have courage to hold out my disability to God for him to use in the way of his choosing. God will be with me wherever I go. I need only to be strong and courageous."

Chapter 8 – The Gift of Joy

"How can we know what joy is without having suffered?"

 "How can we fully know and appreciate joy without having suffered? Joy is born from suffering."

Chapter 9 – The Gift of Community

"How can we know what community is until we make space for others?"

Chapter 10 – The Gift of Transformation

"How can we be formed without carving and chiseling? He is forming us into who he intends us to be."

Chapter 11 – The Gift of Faith

"How can we know how to have faith without learning from others who embody it?"

Chapter 12 – The Gift of Mercy

"How can we know what mercy is until we've practiced gifting it?"

Chapter 13 – The Gift of Repentance

"How can we know what repentance is until we walk toward the cross instead of a comfortable life?"

"Matthew's life changed drastically when he followed the homeless man instead of his wealth. He chose honesty over fraud and humility over prosperity. He walked next to Jesus as a student to learn about this curious upside-down way of life. "

"Matthew chose to be a lowly sheep and gave up his wealth that didn't satisfy. What he gained in his repentance is priceless and eternal."

Chapter 14 – The Gift of Endurance

"How can we know what endurance is without being refined by fire?"

"Jesus likes to give people nicknames, according to who he sees us *becoming*. Like to Simon, he gave the name Peter, meaning the "Rock," even though Peter was not rock-solid. God saw who he was becoming instead of focusing on his weaknesses. And you know what? Peter eventually died a martyr's death for his beloved friend and Savior, and he chose to be crucified upside-down. What kind of faith is more rock-solid than that? He must have had a compelling reason to give his life in this way. He understood the 'why.'"

"We may never know the reason God allows us to endure the flames. Job never understood the 'why' in his suffering. God never told him, even though they conversed. If God had described to Job the reason for his suffering, Job wouldn't have exemplified his faith the way he did by *not* knowing."

"Enduring suffering can become a gift because it is an opportunity for us to grow from who we are into who God intends for us to become."

Chapter 15 – The Gift of Direction

"How can we know what direction to go when we do not have control of our steps? Our plans get thwarted, but from God's perspective, our path always points to him—True North."

"God has worked everything for my good in the past, so when I doubt he will in my future, I must look back and remember his faithfulness."

"Humility is our strength that leaves room for God's grace to be sufficient. There is beauty beyond the thorns—Christ. He has reasons to allow thorns in our lives. Paul wrote more books in the Bible than anyone despite his fleshly thorn. Isn't that beautiful? See how God used Paul's thorn for good? He wants to turn our weaknesses to strengths too."

"Pride is more dangerous than a thorn. If you've been given a thorn, it is for your protection; it has been gifted because there is something beautiful that is being purposed for you. God knows the 'why.' His grace and knowledge are sufficient. You can trust him. Suffering has taught me what matters most in life is not what we see, but what God sees."

Chapter 16 – The Gift of Fulfillment

"How can we know what fulfillment is until we let God alone fill?"

∽ "We try to fill ourselves with things that don't fulfill. Food never fulfills—the lack of it or the overabundance of it."

∽ "Only God is the heart-shaped peg that fits into our heartfelt need."

∽ "True worth isn't found in appearance. We can only find it by believing how God feels about us. In him is where we find our *true* identity."

∽ "Satan and his minion demons try to separate us from God. But don't let them. Fight them with the truth about who and whose you are. Instead of food and other addictions, God's Word can be our go-to comfort."

Chapter 17 – The Gift of Provision

"How can we not know what provision is when God made creation to reproduce fish, fowl, beasts, plants, and trees?"

∽ "God provides for our needs daily. Like his disciples were expected and taught to figure out a way to help meet the needs of the hungry, we too are given the task of helping those who need a hand. We are called to compassion—to notice needs around us and respond in love. God will miraculously multiply our efforts to make a difference in ways we cannot even see."

∽ "God provides us with resources, and he will multiply our efforts, but we must take the step of giving before he can multiply."

Chapter 18 – The Gift of a Shepherd

"How can we understand the gift of our Shepherd if we don't understand the needs of a sheep?"

"We must see people. We must be compassionate. We must reach out and touch others; our efforts will help heal something in those people."

Chapter 19 – The Gift of Touch

"How can we understand the value of touch if we've never held the hand of a sufferer?"

"I find it ironic that Jesus didn't have to touch lepers to heal them, yet he did. His perfect love and compassion touched them because he wanted to initiate their emotional healing, not just their physical recovery."

"Many of us have given up reaching out in faith to 'touch' Jesus. Instead, we are waiting for Jesus to 'touch' us. When we feel he hasn't, we claim he is non-existent or doesn't care. We have a choice: Do we turn toward God in trust, or do we turn away from him in bitterness? Will we remain bitter and angry, or let God reveal himself and his beauty beyond the thorns to us throughout our suffering?"

Chapter 20 – The Gift of Gratitude

"If we don't express gratitude, is it because we feel entitled?"

"Are we so used to God doing things for us we take him for granted? Afflictions in my life have deepened my gratitude for things and people I used to take for granted. Think about a wound you have had in your life, like a skinned knee. God formed new skin cells and healed that wound. Isn't that remarkable? I mean, I can't make new skin cells. Can you? Oh, how often we take our Healer for granted."

Chapter 21 – The Gift of a Good Samaritan

"How can we know how to be a Good Samaritan if we don't allow ourselves to be inconvenienced to help someone in need?"

Chapter 22 – The Gift of Forgiveness

"How can we know what forgiveness is until we have been utterly broken by our sin?"

Chapter 23 – The Gift of Sight

"How can we know what sight is without following the One who sees?"

"You may not understand the whys of your life sufferings, but like Hagar, once you realize God sees you, you can be strengthened to carry on fulfilling your purpose. Living with chronic pain has clarified my purpose. Various callings have been eliminated and illuminated, providing a path I do not question. My purpose hasn't been compromised; it's been defined."

"Once we know God sees us, it will strengthen us to see others more clearly."

Chapter 24 – The Gift of Wholeness

"How can we be whole if we hide behind our pain?"

Chapter 25 – The Gift of Obedience

"If Jesus learned obedience through suffering, how will we?"

"In the classic Sermon on the Mount, Jesus told the listening crowds that life going forward would be backward. Before, kings lived in palaces; now, the King is homeless. Before, the Pharisees dictated the behavior of society; now, the love of God would. Before, those who were sick, outcast, and oppressed were on the fringe; now, they would be honored. Before, victory came from winning wars; now, the war would be won by the Savior of the world dying on a cross. It all seemed so backward because it was. It still is. How many people do you know that consider meekness a strength? Or aspire to be gentle? Or strive to obey God instead of following their desires?"

"How do you honestly feel when you look to embrace the way of life described in the Beatitudes? Poor in spirit. Mourners. Meek. Hungry and thirsty for righteousness. Merciful. Pure in heart. Peacemakers. Persecuted because of righteousness. Insulted. False accusations and evil said against you because of him. Are you willing?"

"Upside-down. Inside out. Backwards. In this world, we are blind, but the Bible can help us see if we listen. The God who sees all does all he can so we also will see."

"We too learn obedience through suffering because it is most often during suffering that we pray and turn to the pages of God's Word, looking for him and answers to life."

Chapter 26 – The Gift of Light

"How can we appreciate the light unless we've encountered despairing darkness?"

"We have been given a light to follow—God. He may seem like a dim taillight to you now, but you will find it becomes brighter the more you follow and invest time and energy into learning about him. The closer you get to him, the more he will illuminate your path, no matter the darkness you have encountered."

Chapter 27 – The Gift of Trust

"How can we understand trust without living humbly?"

"Sad truth is that Satan is remarkably successful at promoting self-rule and autonomy over humility and trust in God. But God didn't create us to be above others or to function self-sufficiently. He made us to have a relationship with him and with others. He made us to value other human beings, not promoting ourselves above another or above him."

"When things are taken from us [like from Job], and we still worship God, we defeat Satan too."

"Like in Job's story, God does not tell us why he allows suffering in our lives. Some of us expect that if God were good, he would give us a comfy life. That is an American tale, not a biblical one."

"Hardening our hearts is a venomous ploy of Satan's, and we are amiss if we listen to his hiss to mistrust the only One who is wholly trustworthy."

Chapter 28 – The Gift of Adoration

"How can we feel God's love if we don't accept his adoration of us?"

"If love is not freely received, it can only go so far before it is obstructed."

"People betray us, tell us we are worthless, use us. Joseph's brothers intended to harm him, but God used his suffering for the good of many people, including saving the lives of his brothers themselves. God adored all of them, and Joseph's thorns ultimately brought glory to God because Joseph adored him."

"To endure suffering is a more extraordinary feat than winning a marathon. The finish line of a marathon is only a steppingstone to more remarkable accomplishments for the sufferer."

Chapter 29 – The Gift of Empathy

"How can we understand the empathy of Christ until we grasp that he himself suffered temptation in every way?"

"…Guess what prepared Jesus for his ministry? Experiencing the wilderness—suffering and thorns. Who better to help those hurting than those who have themselves undergone trials? Without experiencing the thorns in the wilderness, we would have no perseverance, empathy, compassion, understanding, joy, courage, gratitude, or deliverance."

"What other religion has a god who has been willing to suffer and die a horrific death? Jesus was nailed to a cross, hanging naked for hours in front of the crowds. #MeToo. What other god has done this for you and miraculously risen from the dead? #NoOne."

 "Heartache sucks the life out of you unless your life aches for Christ."

Chapter 30 – The Gift of Brokenness

*"How can we find comfort from God in our brokenness
if we don't accept Jesus was pierced for our transgressions?"*

 "All of us are broken. We come from broken families with broken hearts, and we grieve broken dreams. We are broken up with and have breakdowns. We barely break even or are flat broke. Our bones break, and our spirits break. Our houses get broken into, and our skin breaks out. We are broken vessels with a broken compass and no clear direction. We wonder when we will have a breakthrough."

 "Jesus knows brokenness. He understands each brand of brokenness, and he knows our brokenness does not have to be the end of our stories or define us. Life does not end during seasons of brokenness, but it changes us. We can find refuge in the One who broke himself so we can be healed. The benefits of having suffered deliver a superior understanding of the benefits of the cross."

"Jesus had the power to but did not stop the Roman soldiers and others from physically breaking him down. He didn't stop them because he knew *the victory was in the breaking;* the victory was beyond what was physically seen, in the spiritual realm. Reason lies beyond the pain, beyond the thorn, beyond our comprehension. We cannot see what God sees, but if we did, as Timothy Keller says, '… God gives us what we would have asked for if we knew everything that He knows.' God sees the benefits of our pain. Our hardest seasons can become some of our most glorious memories and training ground for our future journey. The past will speak for itself in time. Our hoped-for outcome may never transpire, but we can change our perspective to live for what God is producing in us, instead of focusing on our limited view."

 "Give me a nail or a blanket, and I'll choose the nail any day. The cross provides lasting comfort—the blanket, a temporary fix."

∽ "How can we be overcomers unless we've been underdogs? Finding meaning provides direction in our lives to help us live our life's purpose. If we are to live in the image of God, we are to bear suffering because Jesus did. How do we gain peace? Piece by piece—one moment, one day, one minute, one second at a time."

∽ What do we do when we feel our will is better than his? My will seems safer because it doesn't include chronic pain. But I must remember everything he allows in my life is to lead to one result—the salvation of my soul. I don't have the power to save it. In this pain, I'm sharing in the death, burial, and resurrection of Christ—where darkness meets light."

∽ "His cross was to die for me, my cross is to live for him. Suffering is the rite of passage to deeper communing with him."

∽ "I don't know if I will ever walk again, but I will always walk with him."

∽ "We are broken but have access to a superpower—the Holy Spirit who can guide us through darkness."

∽

Your Reflections

Your Reflections

Your Reflections

About the Author

Darci J. Steiner has served in the ministry as a teen and women's ministry leader, as well as assisted with church plants in Denver and Los Angeles. In 2001, Darci nearly lost her life after a debilitating fall. During her recovery, she earned her Master of Science degree in Holistic Nutrition and implemented natural remedies into her diet that helped save her life. When Darci became disabled a second time in 2018, she turned her focus toward ministry again by writing her debut book, *Beauty Beyond the Thorns: Discovering Gifts in Suffering* and its companion, *Study Guide for Beauty Beyond the Thorns: Discovering Gifts in Suffering*. Darci and her husband live in the Denver area.

www.DarciJSteiner.com

If you enjoyed the *Beauty Beyond the Thorns* book and study guide, kindly leave a review on Amazon to help more people discover gifts in their suffering.
Deeply grateful, Darci.

www.ingramcontent.com/pod-product-compliance
Lightning Source LLC
Chambersburg PA
CBHW081419080526
44589CB00016B/2594